So, Are You Living Happily, Ever After?

So, Are You Living Happily, Ever After?

What do you Do, when your Life isn't working out?

P.A. Pilio

Team PA.Pilio

ISBN-13: 9798664628999

Library of Congress Control Number: 2018675309
Printed in the United States of America

Cover photograph by Team PA.Pilio
Cover design and typesetting by: Team PA.Pilio
Publisher: Team PA.Pilio

OOOOO

For You, Panda

May Your Light Always Shine Bright

And Love Eternal

Table of Contents

You came for the joy of deliberate creation

ooo

You are so free, you can choose bondage

Abraham

Foreword

INDEED, a humbling experience to contribute to this part of P.A.Pilio's (life) story. I am filled with gratitude, awe, and inspiration as a witness to her journey.

Life can be so much more joyful than what we allow! The overall theme of life as a classroom, and the multitude of lessons we face, can be viewed, and experienced from a completely different point of view. One that does not add to the fear of failure in this 'classroom', but to the enjoyment of it. One that allows the 'recess'; the happiness and joy part of this experience on beloved earth.

You are an amazing creator with the capacity and potential for love, abundance, prosperity, and joy. Life is this profound unfolding of events leading us onto this path. And in this process, the essence of who we truly are, becomes apparent. We lean into this essence, embracing this essence, getting to know a completely new version of ourselves. This is the value of this beautifully written book.

P.A. Pilio has truly lived and experienced the path of creation shared here. It is the sharing of events and experiences contributing to many learnings and aha moments in finding this essence, on this path towards enlightenment. The essence of who we truly are shines through her Beingness – credible, truthful, sagacious, and creative, she takes you through finding the same within you.

This is the journey; this is the light in the dark to navigate your way through experiencing: 'So, Are You Living Happily, Ever After?'

Michelle Vooght

" When You Wish Upon A Star,

makes no difference who you are;

Anything Your Heart Desires,

will come to you. "

Walt Disney's 'Pinocchio'

Introduction

DEAR READER, this is not a book in the conventional sense of the world, or the word. Rather, this is a Collection of thoughts, understandings and knowledge gleaned through personal experience.

The subject matter is an approach to life that is fast garnering attention, and hence momentum, across the globe. And this is: The Art of Deliberate Creating. Or, as we shall come to see: The Art of Intentionally Translating Vibration into Matter.

And, if you have been called to read these words, then they will resonate with you. And, will prove to be both of interest, and of value to you.

We shall explore topics such as: Your connection to the Creator-force. Your powerful ability to create whatever you desire. How and why you are creating the life you are living. How to manifest the life that you dream of. The Laws of the Universe. The Law of Attraction. Your role in co-creating All that You Are. Universal expansion. Why you came, and your purpose in life.

We could call this a compilation of Essays, and that's ideal. Because in these words, there is no beginning and no ending. Each chapter stands in *this* moment of understanding.

In the same way, this is also true of you. You too, are never-ending, ever-expanding, in this eternal now

The truth is that:

- You, and only you, are responsible for every single thing that you have ever experienced.

- Through your focus, you are attracting all that you are currently experiencing.

- By directing this focus, you hold the power to choose what you create in your experience tomorrow. And every day thereafter.

All you have lived has brought you right to this moment. To this 'now'. And where you are, despite what you may think, is really just fine. Because nothing needs to be rooted in what-was. And nothing needs to stay the same, in what-is. Because the what-is that you want to reach for, is beyond 'now'.

Which is why, relaxing into where you are, and making the best of it, is actually the first step on your journey to allowing yourself the life you dream of.

I share these words with you, confidently and enthusiastically, because I know them to be accurate and filled with truth.

And, how do I know this?

- Because the thoughts felt good when they were first received.

- The words continue to feel good when they are read.

And this means their resonance is sound, and will not be found wanting.

P.A. Pilio

YOUR JOURNEY NEVER ENDS

We are eternal. We come from Source energy. We are, each and every-one, part of the Creator-force.

WE are an extension of the Aether referred to in ancient languages and teachings, whether alchemical or secular. The vastness that is undefined. The 'No-thing-ness that is All'. The Ain Suph Aur that is no-thing and all-things.

Like a bee hive or ants' nest, the decision to come is a collective one. Operating collectively, whilst we were still all together, we chose. We choose through our intention. Our No-thing intention to become some-thing.

In this universe, that is a universe fashioned on a platform of attraction, our undivided focus on our intention to come, to manifest into physical form, gathers momentum. Gathers energetic form, that becomes thought, that becomes physical form.

There is no stark opposition of Higher thing to Lower thing. Nor of Better to Less-better. There is no separation between Divine and Mundane. Nor between Omnipotent and Vulnerable. There is no line that separates Magical from Ordinary. We are all One.

We are all One.

You came because the Universe's sole drive is self-perpetuation. Self-perpetuation's sole intention is expansion. Every-thing culminates in Expansion. In the expansion, the self-perpetuation of the Universe.

And it is contrast, it is variety and diversity, that drives expansion. Because contrast drives choice, that in turn drives desire.

And that is why you, the part of non-physical energy that came, stand now in physical form. To facilitate, to lead the expansion of the universe. And the way you intended to do this, is through the process of joyful co-creation.

But wait, let's go back a moment. And you can. Go back. Look back. Because that's something you in physical form can do. And oh boy, do you do it.

But, the greater part of you that remained in energetic, non-physical form, never looks back. The focus, the attention, the singular interest, the intent of the non-physical part that is you, is always on the vision you hold for your future.

Your Guiding-self never looks back. Because that's already done. The expansion has already taken place.

That's old news. In its very manifestation, it is already done.

The new expansion lies in your most current desires. Those that are still a dream, a hope, a prayer, a wish.

LET'S BEGIN AGAIN

Together, Non-physical energy – Universal Consciousness, the
Aether, the God-Head – desired expansion.

AND, this non-physical energy had an intention, a plan. Part of this amorphous mass would separate and came into physical form – the physical you, and you, and you, and you – to experience the contrast that our planet offers.

There is contrast in every molecule in our universe. That which is both wanted, and unwanted. However, the expansive variety and diversity we have access to, ensures that this is far greater on Earth.

The intention of the greater part of universal consciousness that remained non-physical, was thus: Variety would lead you, in physical form, to exercise a choice, a preference.

And in exercising your preference, you would ask for what you wanted. Like an artist, you would hand craft, you would fashion your desire. And each desire would be like no other in the universe. Unique solely unto you.

And the expression of that desire, the vibration of it, would burst forth into the aether.

Instantaneously, the non-physical part of you would align vibrationally with the purity of that desire. And, in experiencing the vibrational actuation of that desire, would remain steadfastly focused on it.

Then, together with the universal Law of Attraction, they would attract the people, places, events, and circumstances necessary to bring that desire, that wanting, into physical manifestation. And they would, unceasingly, intuit to you, the best way for you to accomplish this manifestation into your physical reality.

◆◆◆◆◆◆

So, you come into physical form, and life comes to you.

Oftentimes you think it is actually coming *at* you, but it really isn't. Our planet lies in a universe of attraction. Only attraction. There is no assertion. Nor is there any exclusion. Only attraction. And inclusion.

Whilst others can impact you, they can do so *only* if you allow it. And the way you allow it, usually without awareness, is by resonating at their frequency; at the frequency of their thoughts, their desires, their beliefs. In other words, by being a match to their vibration.

So, here you are, experiencing life. Or rather, experiencing the variety and diversity that life offers. All the daily experiences comprising the ups and downs; the highs, and lows; what you think of as the good and bad; the joy and sorrows; the boredom and over-excitement. Both ends of the stick, so to say, and everything in between. And there is certainly an abundance of sticks from which you can choose.

Yet with remarkable ease, you set about sifting and sorting, and deliberating and deciding, and choosing and not choosing – that is also a choice – and coming to conclusions about what you like and what you don't like. What you prefer to have and what you'd rather not have.

And nothing makes you more clear in knowing what you *do* want, than when you experience something that you *don't* want.

Because when you experience something that feels a little off, or perhaps feels bad, or perhaps feels awful, with a jolt of absolute clarity, you know precisely what you'd rather experience.

And in the act of making that decision, a powerful desire is born within you. That is the next step in the process of creating. In the process of becoming. In the process of expansion.

Herein lies the value in all that is unwanted: If you never experience unwanted, you would never know the pleasure of experiencing the wanted. It is as if the one gives birth to the other.

Unwanted causes you to want. And that desire causes the expansion of the non-physical part of you. And if it all goes according to plan, the further expansion of you, too.

So, whether or not you vocalise, or even acknowledge this new desire, in *that* moment of clarity, you gave life to this brain-child.

You birthed a new vibrational emanation.

And the greater part of you, that remained in non-physical, immediately attaches to this energetic new-form, and expands into it. And then holds it in their undivided attention.

Your Guiding-self[1] matches the vibration of the pure positivity of your new physical **wanting**.

You see, your Guiding-self enjoys a complete, detailed overview of everything: Knows where you are physically; knows where you are vibrationally; knows where your desire is vibrationally. And beams to you the directions to your desire. Moment-by-moment.

Wherever you currently stand, there are any number of routes you could take that would lead you to your desire. And your Guiding-self knows each and every one. So, as you turn this way, you are guided on this new route. And should you turn that way, you are guided along that route.

Always along the route that is the easiest for you. And the most enjoyable that you will allow yourself to follow.

There is never only a singular way to attain what you want. Never ever. Your ship never sails without you. Nor, can you ever 'miss the boat'. For the simple reason that there is a never-ending stream of boats waiting for you to hop aboard, at any one time. And if this one sails, then another will fill its place. And another. And more.

---

[1] The Non-physical part of you is referred to variously as your Soul, your Spirit, your Essential Self, your Higher Self, your I Am Presence, your Animating principal, your Inner Being.

We call this part of you, your Guiding-self, because this is a familiar activity that can be readily identified with: Being guided. And this expansive non-physical part of you, could in any moment be: Your prosperity guide, your vitality guide, your animal guide, your angel guide, your spirit guide, your guardian angel; your master-teacher. In other words: All that is part of the Creator-force. And everything that you identify with, as Being such.

Your Guiding-self is the 'Whole' of who you are. This pure positive energy adores you; is focussed upon you at all times; knows everything about you; knows your every secret and every desire; and knows how best to lead you forward in the joyful expansion you intended.

Because this non-physical part of you, never stops transmitting directions to you – through impulses, through thoughts, through ideas, through what you may term intuition. Through other people, through rendezvous, through events.

In other words:

- Initially, non-physical you, leads you into physical form.

- Then you birth a desire, and your Guiding-self instantaneously attracts to that vibrational new wanting.

- And your Guiding-self expands into, and holds the vibration of this new part of you. And then sets about nudging you to it.

Like carefully laying cookies on a trail, your Guiding-self [2] never stops broadcasting to you, and guiding you to what you want – to the life that you desire.

____

[2] Your Guiding-self is not separate from you. You, and non-physical You, are One. And when you come to acknowledge this, and accept this, so much more will fall into place. Because the art of deliberate creating, is actually the art of vibrationally melding you, with non-physical you.

FORGOTTEN, NOT LOST

But many have forgotten that we intended to dance, this eternal dance, together.

MANY have forgotten how we intended to lead one another in this glorious dance of co-creation.

How you would come and sift and sort through the variety, desire some-thing, and emanate that desire. And that your Guiding-self would then hold that vibration and call you to it.

And how, in aligning with the higher vibration that *is* your non-physical-self, you would come to match that vibration.

In doing so, your thoughts, through the momentum of your focus and the magnetism of attraction, would ultimately bring about the realization of the physical manifestation of that thing.

So, how do we forget?

- We forget because we are taught otherwise by the well-intentioned people who love us, and the well-meaning people who 'teach' us.

- Instead of encouraging you to remain connected to the high energetic vibration that you are when you arrived; instead of focusing on your joy, and love, and abundance, that resonate at that vibration, you are taught to care about what others think and what others feel and what others say and what others do.

    o   So, you take your focus away from the 'All' that you know you are. And you over-shadow this with fitting in. With being liked. With wanting to please. With getting on with others. With putting them, and their desires first. And, in doing so, you sublimate the whole of who you are.

In sublimating your own desires; your own joy; your own happiness, you separate yourself from that vibration of love and abundance that you are eternally. And in this separation, you no longer 'hear' the calling of that non-physical part of you.

The longer this goes on, the more miserable you become. Because no matter where you are in this experience of life, there is an inner knowing that you just aren't meant to experience those feelings of dissatisfaction, or despair, or hopelessness, or anger, or hurt, or jealousy, or blame, or worthlessness. It feels rotten.

You just know that something is off. But you don't know what it is. Because you don't remember that you did not intend to fly this life solo. You also don't recall how to re-connect with the Whole of who you are.

All the while, the more we move away, the worse we feel. Until we come to the point where we bury ourselves in whatever we can find that soothes: Substances, prescribed or not; excessive physical activity; distractions; work. We push ourselves further. Harder. We hurt ourselves, we hurt those we love. We break apart our relationships. We even go to war.

We go to war against any-thing from drunk drivers to religion to race, to sexual preference to political preference to rudeness, to carbohydrates to disinterest. We go to war against people who choose differently to us. We go to war against climate change, against carbon emissions, against drugs, against movies, against books, against our neighbour's dog. The list is constantly changing, and truly never-ending.

Yet, in this universe of attraction, you can never fix anything that you push against. And, just for the record – there is nothing here, that *ever* needs fixing.

And you certainly didn't come with the purpose of making anything 'right'. Because the variety and the diversity contained within life, is the very essence of what causes you to choose, and to desire, and to add to the expansion that you are.

In other words: Everything is perfectly the way it is. And from this magnificent and extensive assortment before you, you intended to choose that which you wanted. You did not intend to focus on what you did not want.

For the simple reason that you knew you cannot change, nor can you fix, anything that you say 'No' to. Irrespective of intention, cause, or justification.

Why can you not change that which you don't like?

- Because in fighting for whatever it is that you choose; in standing up for whatever it is that you feel passionately about, you are always fighting *against* something else.

- You're choosing *this* over *that*. And in doing so, you rarely focus upon what you're actually wanting. Instead, your focus lies on rejecting, on wanting to push away that other, contrasting thing.

- And when you place your attention over there, on whatever it is that you don't want, the way you feel about it causes you to find vibrational harmony with it.

- In other words, the emotions you experience when you think about it, or look at it, or talk about it, or watch it, cause you to come to resonate with the very topic, or atti-tude, or situation that you are railing against.

o   And you cannot improve anything from that lower vibra-tion. Because in steps the Law of Attraction.

OUR UNIVERSAL MANAGER

The Law of Attraction is the non-discriminating manager of all vibrations within our universe.

IN essence, the law of attraction is responsible for bringing together vibrations that resonate at a similar frequency. The frequencies of things unseen, hence non-physical. And the vibrations of that which is not yet physically manifested.

Imagine streams of energy flowing through the universe, like contrails through the sky. But rather than comprising visible ice particles, these are invisible streams of energy, that together comprise every single thought, that has ever been thought. Every thought, and hence every idea, and belief, and hope, and prayer, and wish.

Each of these streams of energy, is amassed and aggregated through attraction, according to the nature of the energetic footprints of those thoughts.

In the same way that we tend to categorise everything – strong and weak, left and right, happy, and sad, rich, and poor, love and hate – the Law of Attraction gathers thoughts according to the energetic vibration at which they resonate.

And because thoughts and emotions are intricately linked – the vibration giving rise to the thought that instantaneously gives rise to the emotion that fuels the thought – feelings are gathered, along with their corresponding thoughts.

Let us take a closer look:

If you're thinking about something you enjoy, these positive thoughts will have you feeling happy, content, pleased, satisfied. Alternatively, if you're contemplating someone that you find irksome, those more negative thoughts will have you feeling frustrated, angered, upset, or piqued.

In the same way, a feeling of contentment will lead to you a thought that matches this finer, positive vibration. Whilst your feelings of anger, that carry a heavier, more dense vibration, will soon have you pondering vibrationally corresponding experiences that elicit negative feelings.

So, we could equally define a range of feelings, and a range of thoughts, that calibrate to the frequency of one another.

These would range from hatred to fear to hopelessness to revenge to rage to frustration to hopefulness to believing to trusting to knowing, all the way to love. Hatred being on one end of the spectrum, love on the other end, with a range of feelings between these two seeming opposites.

Now, there are other emotions that are similar in feeling to those mentioned.

For example:

- We could put powerlessness together with hopelessness.

- Boredom could fit with both frustration and pessimism.

- Joy and knowing and optimism really feel good.

- Whilst despair feels about as bad as fear.

This is just what the law of attraction does. It brings together similarly resonating thoughts and feelings.

Therefore, in any circumstance when you say 'No' to what you don't want, you may as well be saying 'Yes' to it.

Because your very focus upon the subject that you want to get rid of, or change, attracts to you more thoughts, and more feelings, and more words, and more people, and more events, that match those same unwanted vibrations.

And the greater the specificity of your focus; the more pointed your intention; the more passionate you are about the subject, the more powerful is the impetus of attraction.

This being the case – and it is – just how then, do you think you're ever going to reach a place of joy and abundance and vitality, when you're surrounding yourself with a growing vibration of what you don't want?

Quite simply, you cannot.

It is not possible for you to achieve your happily, ever after, when:

- You're mired in the negativity of that which you do not want.

- You are predominantly focussed on the absence of what you want.

- You're feeling hard done by, or depressed, or worried, or agitated, or confused, or any of the other negative emotions you may experience on a moment-by-moment basis.

The only way you can facilitate the manifestation of your happily ever after, is to have 'a spring in your step'. To be Happy.

To feel abundant, and eager, and expectant of those wanted things coming. To be clear of mind, and looking forward to what tomorrow will bring.

This is the only way of Being that will get you from where you presently are, to where you want to go.

It is not possible to get to there, from a place of feeling lack, or frustration, or any other negative emotion. This, no matter how much you want to, nor how hard you try.

In order to reach where you're wanting to go, *you must shift yourself vibrationally*. You have to find a way to move yourself up that emotional scale. Bit-by-bit.

One step at a time.

WHAT DO YOU WANT?

In this universe of attraction, you get what you focus on. Always.
And every time.

WHICH is the reason for the Art of Deliberate Creation, being premised upon you giving your attention, to that which you want. And not to that which you don't want.

Well, that sounds simple enough. But not, when you consider how much time is spent going around in circles, questioning: Should I do this, or is it better for me to do that? Oh, perhaps this way is better? If I do that, how will it affect them? What will happen if I choose this, instead? Should I, shouldn't I? Could I, couldn't I? Argh!

So, let us begin by asking: "What is the one thing each and every one on this planet wants?"

"Oh, hold on there", you may say, "we all come from different backgrounds and cultures and experiences. How can we all possibly want the same thing? In any event, he wants robust health; she wants to build an empire; I want respect; they want a beautiful home; she wants a partner; he wants love, and of course we all want more money."

Yes, this is so. But, underlying each and every desire, of each and every one, is a single, common driving force. And that is: The desire to feel better.

For much of the time, and from whatever place you are in, you are fuelled by the desire to feel better than you do right now. And you largely believe that you will feel better, when you attain those objects that you desire.

Yet, you are sorely mistaken in the belief that happiness lies in the having of things. Afterall, if and when you do finally get that item you've been wanting, how often does the initial effervescence of receiving it, all too quickly fade?

Almost all the time.

Why is this?

- o   Well, certainly not because 'you're never satisfied'.

- o   And certainly not because 'you're greedy'.

- o   And certainly not because 'you want too much'.

Not for any of those limiting beliefs circulating in your mind.

In fact, your satisfaction with what comes in the moment, is entirely natural. Because your satisfaction happens in the moment. In the now, and in the now, and now.

You are an extension of the Creator-force. You are an eternal creator. And to be permanently satisfied is counter to your very Being.

So, your satisfaction with what-is, *must* be temporal. Because, together with the expansion precipitated by the appearance of this new subject of your desire, through its very manifestation, you are presented with more variety and more diversity.

And this new variety and new diversity, once again contains that which is both unwanted, and wanted. That again causes new desire to birth within you. And the process of creating starts again, and again, and again. Precisely as you intended.

Because this is how the non-physical part of you expands. This is how the universe expands. And ultimately, this is how you expand.

Children inherently know this. Which is why:

- They believe the world revolves them. Because it does.

- They want it now. Because they know that's how it's meant to be.

- They move onto the next thing quickly. Because their constant desire to create leads them there.

Then well-intentioned parents and elders spend years teaching this out of them.

So, you set your eyes on this new object, or happening. And, after the initial thrill at its arrival, arguments start in the new relationship, or you now want the car to go faster, or the new job actually isn't stimulating, or the money still isn't enough.

All too soon, you find yourself looking to something else to make you feel better. And in this way, you get bound-up in a self-perpetuating cycle of wanting-waiting-joy-or disappointment. Wanting-waiting-joy-or disappointment.

Joy if it comes. Disappointment when it does not. As is the case, more often than not.

And the reason for it not coming, is because you cannot manifest outside of your 'now-vibration'. So, on those occasions when you happen to get out of your own way, you may get it right, and that item comes. But mostly, you do not. And so, the emotional roller-coaster ride continues.

But if I set my goal on what I want, and remain focussed on it; if I talk-the-talk until I can walk-the-walk. Surely then I'll get what I want?

Maybe you could. After you've worked hard, and struggled and sacrificed.

We're just suggesting you take an easier route. And, once you know how, that you enjoy yourself along the way.

Because having things does not, and never will bring you happiness.

For these logical reasons:

- You live in a universe where vibration, and not action, is king.

- And so, you have first and foremost, *to find the vibration of what it is you're wanting.*

- As everything you want is because you believe you will feel better in the having of it, the vibration you're after is one of *feeling better in each moment.*

In other words, just get happy.

Once you do, the Law of Attraction will bring to you more and more and more that resonates at this higher frequency.

You see, you don't attract happiness through things. But oh, when you realize that you *do* attract things *through* your happiness ...... Well now, that's the stuff of deliberate creating.

Then, rather than that self-perpetuating emotional roller-coaster ride of wanting-waiting-joy-or disappointment, you can achieve a place of clarity and stability.

When you are leading through how you are feeling, moment-by-moment, you are able to intentionally shift yourself up that emotional scale. And as you start feeling better, you start attracting to you, more that feels better.

Until, in not too long a time at all, you could find yourself enjoying a place of wanting-believing-expecting-receiving. Wanting-believing-expecting-receiving.

I WANT IT ALL

"I want happier relationships, more money, a fulfilling career, but nothing ever seems to change for me."

BECAUSE, as things presently stand, you look at what's around you, and believe that: "If I can just get this one object, the world will look bright, and I'll feel great".

You think that the car, or the house, or the lover or the sense of security, or the career or the health, or the money – yes, so often the money – is all that you need, for your life to turn around.

So, you work and wait and want. And you wait and want and work, some more. But you still don't see that object of your desire.

And your frustration grows at your wanting and working and waiting. Until you cry out, "I know what I want. I'm doing all I can. Why can't I get it?"

Well, the short answer is: You can. And, in a sense, you do. Every single time.

Your asking is answered in the precise moment that you birth that desire.

The fact that you cannot see it, or hear it, or taste it, or touch it, or smell it, is not evidence that is does not exist. Because it does. It has come into Vibrational Being.

It's up to you, to then *consciously* interpret the expanded-ness of it. In other words: It's up to you to translate the vibration of it, and to bring into physical manifestation, that which you desire.

The way you accomplish this is by improving how you feel, so as to raise your own vibration, in order to tune-in to your Guiding-self.

Remember how, through its variety and diversity, life prompts you to choose, and hence to desire. And that once that desire emanates from you, your Guiding-self holds fast to that vibration and calls you to it, through ideas, thoughts, impulses, rendezvous, and people?

Well, this *really* is happening all the time. It is occurring in every 'now' moment. Your Guiding-self is constantly beaming to you all you need to know, in order for you to move towards your happily, ever after.

Yet, 'back at the ranch', what are *you* doing?

Probably, not much. Not much that is helpful in your pursuit of happiness.

You wake in the morning, go about your preparations, think about the mildly unpleasant encounter you had last week, hope you get that phone call or invitation, recall the unsettling news you heard yesterday, wonder if things are going to work out today, pray that they will, worry about what might happen if they don't.

And that's all before 09:00!

So just where, in all this muddle of thinking – in all this busyness and concern – have you allowed the space, even for a moment, to receive anything? Let alone a prompting from the Universe: A thought or an impulse from your Guiding-self.

With all this interference going on, how can anything of this fine energetic footprint possibly get through to you?

Quite simply: Nothing that should, can.

So: Nothing that should, does.

And often this leaves you in a lonely place. Because:

- o   In the physical absence of that which you are wanting, and;

- o   In your not believing in the veracity of the vibrational manifestation of all you have asked for, both in this lifetime and before;

- o   You've come to believe that if you work hard and struggle and suffer, some benevolence will eventually, if you're good, smile down on you and somehow make things better.

◆◆◆◆◆◆

This is a universe of attraction. This is *not* a universe of assertion. Your benevolence, that is your Guiding-self, cannot force you to do anything, or to go anywhere. Nor can they lead you to where you *do* want to go, if you are not open to receive their guidance.

In order to receive their guidance, that is flowing to you constantly and consistently, you have to find a way to calibrate yourself to that higher frequency from whence your Source is broadcasting to you.

In other words: You have to be tuned-in to their band-width.

In much the same way, if you want to listen to mellow late-night tunes on your favourite app, it would be of no help to you whatsoever, if you were to download the sounds of a heavy metal artist.

You need to selectively choose the broadcast you want to listen to. You must 'tune-in' to the broadcast of those soundwaves that you wish to receive.

In just the same way, you must selectively tune-in to the frequency that your Guiding-self resonates at.

This frequency, is the highest and finest of all. It is the resonance of pure positivity. It is the vibration of pure Love. And of Satisfaction, and of Clarity, and of Joy, and of Abundance, and of Vitality, and of Passion, and of Enthusiasm, and of Compliments, and of Eagerness, and of Compassion, and of Prosperity. It is the vibration of that which feels wonderful.

Now, we're not saying that this is where *you* always ought to be. *This* is where that non-physical part of you always is.

And when you get in this vicinity, you will tune-in to their broadcasts. You will receive their guidance. You will be able to pick up the delicious cookies that you'll find all along your path through life.

Just how do you tune-in?

o   Your mind is your broadcaster.

o   Your mind is also your receiver.

o   And the only way to selectively tune your mind, is by shutting out all other broadcasts. By eliminating all interference. All distractions. All static.

o   You must quieten your mind.

In so doing, you allow your mind to clearly receive those broadcasts, those promptings, that the greater non-physical part of you is beaming to you in a never-ending pattern of love.

QUIETEN YOUR MIND

The starting point in this process of allowing yourself to receive,
is meditation. Because nothing quietens the mind
more effectively.

NOW, some may think of meditation as a challenge. As something that is difficult to accomplish. However, when you approach it lightly and simply, mediation really is within your reach.

Regular practice is essential to the process of conscious creation, as this steadily compounds the improvement in your vibration. So, let us share with you how to incorporate meditation into your daily routine.

- Should you wish to set a timer, do so.

- Then, gently shake your body loose, for a few seconds. This helps to bring your focus inward.

- Now, make yourself comfortable: Sit in a chair with your feet on the floor, and your hands comfortably resting in your lap. You may prefer to sit cross-legged on a cushion, with your hands resting on your thighs.

Alternatively, you may wish to lie down. But preferably not if you suspect you'll fall asleep. Your thoughts are arrested when you sleep, so this is a good option when you want to stop momentum around negative thinking. However, the benefit of the shift in your vibration through quietening your mind, will be lost.

- Begin by stating your intention for quietening your mind. One simple sentence spoken out loud: "I am now quietening my mind in order to allow my connection to All that I Am".

You are not quietening your mind with the purpose of receiving answers to questions. You are not quietening your mind in order to receive nudges. Nor to find out more about this, or to know more about that. You are not even quietening your mind with the explicit intention of raising your vibration.

This is not a practise motivated by reward. The end-goal is simply to gently quieten your beautiful mind, and allow your connection with the Whole of Who You Are.

Your mind is not the enemy. It is not something to be overcome or conquered. Your mind is part of the eternal flow; part of that exhilarating dance that you and your non-physical partner are eternally engaged in.

- Now, simply place your attention on the rhythmic in-and-out of your breathing.

  - You may find it of benefit to count while you breathe: In for four counts, and out for four counts.

  - An interesting option is to inhale to the count of three, and exhale either to the count of five, or to the sound in your mind of 'Aum', or 'Om'. This change in pace requires your mind to focus here, a little more, and so can be of benefit.

  - Alternatively, you may prefer to focus on the gentle sound of a clock ticking, or on the tinkling of water, or on the white noise of an appliance – such as the sound of a fan, or an air-conditioner.

o   There are also apps, with a useful fade-out timer, that offer the sounds of birds and falling rain and thunderstorms and frogs, and more. Just don't choose a sound that piques your interest, like that of a waterfall, that then reminds you of that fabulous ... and off goes that thinking mind of yours, like a runaway train.

Choose whichever works best for you, and then focus on this calming, repetitive, not-so-interesting sound for a while each morning.

- You don't need to meditate for an arduous stretch of time. 15-20 minutes a day will do beautifully. However, if you feel like sitting for a little longer because you're feeling good, then of course do so.

- And wake a little earlier each day, so you can quieten your mind before your day begins.

Why before your day begins?

Because when you sleep, you stop thinking. And when you stop thinking, the energy that is moving around those thoughts, and the attraction that brings more to you, is suspended.

So, shortly after awakening – whilst you pick up with your vibration right where you left it the night before – it is easier to quieten your mind. There is less static. Less background noise. You mind is less active.

Whereas later in the day, your mind is again racing along with everything you've been doing, and encountering, and thinking. And quietening the momentum of all this, is more difficult to accomplish.

It goes without saying: Do not try to quieten your mind when time is an issue, nor if you have some pressing matter to attend to. It will not work. Your attempt will yield only frustration.

Rather come back and sit again tomorrow morning.

And the morning after that. And the morning after that.

- Sometimes, a hurdle to settling into the practise of daily morning meditation, is wondering "Is it working"? Or, "Am I doing this right"?

  You have an inkling that it's working, when your start to feel a sort of gentle dis-connect from your body. As if you can't really discern one body part from another. You just feel rather 'even' all over.

  You could also experience a 'lightness', or a sensation of floating.

With time, you may also feel a subtle tingling or buzzing somewhere in your body, or a gentle involuntary movement in an extremity. If you do, you can be assured that's you, saying 'hi' to you.

◆ ◆ ◆ ◆ ◆ ◆

So, there you are, resting comfortably, focussed on the rhythmic sound you've selected, when you suddenly realize that you're no longer focussing on it, at all. You're thinking about something that happened, or something you must do, or something you should not have done, or the appointment you need to make, or any one of a million other things.

Relax. Your mind got bored, and wandered. That's all. Nothing has gone wrong. Afterall, the very purpose of your mind is to think. Its function is to sift and sort through data, and to analyze.

Yet now you're asking your mind to be quiet. To stop doing what it does best. And this is going to require a little patience, and perseverance, but you *will* get there.

How can you be sure?

Because thousands of thousands, just like you, have successfully incorporated meditation into their daily routine.

So, when you catch yourself thinking, just let the thought pass you by. As if you're sitting on a park bench and watching the world go by.

Now you see it. Now you don't anymore.

Just softly bring your attention back to that gentle rhythmic sound.

But sometimes, no sooner do you re-focus, than your mind goes off on another trajectory again. This time, perhaps wondering how long you've been sitting. Again, just let the thought pass you by, and bring your attention back to that rhythmic sound.

Every time you notice yourself thinking about something, just let it flow past you.

It will be this way for a time. But gradually you'll find your mind, both wondering and wandering less. It will start to become a little quieter, for a little longer. You will find yourself thinking less. And all you need do, to achieve this, is practice a little.

Practice gently.

Practice softly.

No pressure.

Practice every day.

Not because you need to, but because you want to.

Because it feels good to chill, and tune-in to what matters.

Like any muscle you want to exercise into shape, you need to exercise your mind into shape, too. Into a different type of shape to what it is accustomed to.

YOU SHALL RECEIVE

As you practise quietening your mind every morning, you will start feeling a sense of satisfaction.

SATISFACTION that comes from realizing that you are deliberately setting aside this time, for the sole purpose of allowing time for you, and you.

Satisfaction in embarking on a new way of Being. You are inviting the connection between you, and your greater non-physical partner. And in your wholeness, lies the access to all that you desire.

As you practice quietening your mind, you are preparing the ground work for your happily, ever after. Because when your mind is quiet, there are no resistant thoughts. And when you are not thinking resistant thoughts, you are paving the way to hearing the promptings from your all-knowing, Guiding-self.

Although, it's not a 'hearing', per say. It's more akin to a thought, or an idea suddenly popping into your mind. Out-of-the-blue, as it were. But not out-of-the-blue. Direct to you from non-physical.

The one common denominator in all you receive from your Guiding-self, is that these nudges are *always* accompanied by a positive, compelling feeling.

The thing is that you are always in the mode of receiving. Which means, that at any point in time, you could be receiving from your Guiding-self. Or you could be receiving from the energy generated around your own positive thoughts and feelings. Your own sense of Well-Being.

But you could also be receiving from:

- Others around you.

- The streams of thought swirling through the universe.

- The energy of the prevailing mass consciousness.

- Your own non-supporting beliefs and negative emotions.

This is why your awareness is so important. Awareness not about why you are receiving, from wherever you are receiving. This could lead you down endless what-ifs. But awareness that, if it makes you feel anything less than good, this is a sure-fire signal for you to change what you're giving your attention to.

Through your focus, and hence through your vibration, you are *always* attracting that which comes to you. In other words: You are *always* choosing from which source you are receiving. However, you are probably doing so by default. We want you to now start doing so, with intent.

And it's really useful to know, that when you align with the frequency of your Guiding-self[3]; when thoughts, ideas, images, suggestions come to you from this pure positive energy, they only ever carry the highest resonance of love.

---

[3] Your Guiding-self knows everything about you, knows precisely what you want, and knows the best way to lead you there.

This greater part of you sees everything you see, hears everything you hear, but never judges you and has no expectation of you. Rather, they simply hold the energetic vibration of pure positivity, and call you to it, eternally.

If what you are receiving feels anything less than this, then you are *not* receiving from your Guiding-Self. It's actually rather straight-forward, you see.

◆ ◆ ◆ ◆ ◆ ◆

Let us return to where you are still sitting comfortably:

And a thought materializes: You suddenly hit upon this great idea. Or you may suddenly feel the impulse to do something, or to speak to someone, or to go somewhere. What this means, is that in your non-resistant state, you opened yourself to receive a prompting from your Guiding-self.

With daily meditation, this could happen within a few days of starting. You could quieten your mind for just a minute, which is long enough for you to receive a nudge.

But know that what you receive is not going to be earth-shattering. It's highly unlikely you're going to receive those winning lottery ticket numbers, nor details of the time and place where you'll meet your new partner.

It is far more likely that the idea that pops into your mind, has seemingly no bearing on anything happening in your life. You may be inspired to simply pick-up a latte. And the thought of doing so feels like a good one.

Well, go and fetch the latte. Because, who knows who'll you meet along the way, or what billboard you may read, or what experience will prompt you to the next idea or rendezvous.

Who knows?

Your Guiding-self knows. That's who knows!

Perhaps, as your meditation draws to a close, you may feel the urge to phone a particular person, and the thought of doing so is appealing. Or you may be inspired to clear out your garage cabinets, and that idea feels compelling. Or an image of something may pop into your mind, that prompts you to eagerly explore further.

The importance of what you receive lies not in the magnitude of the thought. Nor in what you perceive to be the appropriateness of the idea, given your current life experience.

Rather, the importance lies in ensuring you act upon this inspiration that you have received. However lowly or trivial the thought may seem.

Do not debate the pros and cons.

Instead of your usual analyzing and doubting, become a partner in the process of your expansion.

- "Why should I follow these compelling, good-feeling thoughts", you ask?

  o Because, as you act on these nudges, and follow the cookie-trail that your Guiding-self is meticulously laying out for you, your trust in your connection with your non-physical partner will grow.

    And in little time, there will be no room for doubt. And that's right where you want to be.

  o Because, as you act on the inspiration you receive, and partner in the unfolding, more of the good stuff will reveal itself to you. More and more of what you want will come into your life, as you feel your way along your personal path of intentional creating.

As you start to consciously notice the connection, between:

- Birthing a desire;

- Being still, and quietening your mind;

- Receiving a prompting from your non-physical partner;

- Acting on this inspiration;

- Witnessing its full unfolding, and receiving the manifestation of your desire.

Then you begin to *know* – not to hope for, not to wish for, but to know – that you are:

• Truly the 'Master of Your Own Universe';

• Being guided every step of the way along your path of creating.

And, with this knowing, also comes the realization that:

• You *can* receive this guidance.

Yes, you are special, and yes you truly are adored. And yes, you have the ability to tune in to your Guiding-self. Anywhere. Any time.

You have a perfect, purposefully designed tool to achieve this connection: Meditation.

So, quieten your mind. It's wholly within your power to do so. Every morning.

And when this knowing embraces you warmly, then you eagerly begin to join the dots on your path to having, being, and doing, anything and everything that you want.

KNOW THY THOUGHTS

Your always-intention should be to: Calibrate yourself towards the frequency of your Guiding-self.

BECAUSE it is here, that all your thought creations are. And in order to receive them, you must raise your vibration to where they are. And the way for you to align to this higher vibration, most effectively, is through meditation.

But that's not where it ends. This is merely the beginning. Because you also want to hold a higher vibration when you are not mediating for those 15-20 minutes each morning. You want to intentionally fashion for yourself, a lasting, happier way of Being.

You want to mould for yourself, a positive bubble of energy, that you can then step out in, and into the world.

You want to have fun. You want to feel enthusiastic, and eager, and interested, and vital. Not just occasionally. Not just when you're engaged in certain activities. Not only when you're with certain friends.

You want to feel this way for as much of the time as possible. And you achieve this by training yourself to be:

- Conscious of your thoughts;

- Aware of how you are feeling;

- Adjusting to feeling better, accordingly.

We live our lives largely in a blur of thinking and activity. Thinking and acting and doing and thinking. And, too often it becomes exhausting.

Acting wears you down. Action can wear you out. Especially as you usually take action when you want something. And that action requires effort.

And *efforting* lies at the opposite end of the spectrum of deliberate creating.

Our physical reality suggests: If you want something, you have to work to get it. Figuratively-speaking, it's all about 'blood, sweat and tears'. But take a look around you, at all the people who are working the hardest, and who predominantly have the least. Yet, those who know how, work little and have much. This is not perchance. It's because the very act of efforting keeps you where you are. Whereas believing in your, as yet, unseen dreams, leads you right to them.

Efforting keeps you where you are, because it keeps you focussed on where you are. In other words, you remain acutely aware of the absence of the things you want.

As you work longer hours, or sit in the traffic, or on that long commute, you are reminded of why you are doing so – to be able to get the things you don't have. And as you examine your bank balance, you are reminded of the stress of your job, and the non-commensurate financial reward, that's not helping you to get there.

You don't have the answer as to how you're going to get off this unsatisfactory treadmill of working and wanting. And no one seems to have the answer. And if you can't come up with a plan, you're going to be doing this forever. And then you'll *never* get those things you so want ... and still don't have.

Do you see? Your hard work keeps you focussed on the lack in your life.

Every day, your efforting reminds you of the life you want, but see no possible way of attaining. All you are aware of, is the absence of what you desire stretching across your future.

And, as we are discovering, you can never get to there, from here. You can never get to where you want to be, from your focus on a place where you do *not* want to be.

So, What *do* you Do, when you Life's not working out?

Why, you become a deliberate creator, of course.

This translates into understanding that:

- You don't need to work and sacrifice and struggle, to make your dreams come true.

- You do need to believe in your dreams.

- You do need to align with your dreams.

- You do need to believe that you are worthy to receive what you are dreaming about.

Then, your dreams will come true. They must. It's law.

◆ ◆ ◆ ◆ ◆

If this resonates with you, and you want to become the deliberate creator you came to be, you absolutely must take hold of what you're thinking-feeling. Because your thoughts become things.

Stated differently: You create what you think about.

So, just how *do* thoughts turn to things?

- In vibrational reality, your thought creations are being held by your Guiding-self, and law of attraction has already gathered to, and added to them. They have become. They are. Fully created. Finito. Done.

- Whilst here in physical reality, your higher vibrational attention to your desires, meaning your thoughts and feelings about them, coupled to the positive expectation you hold for them, attracts similarly resonating thoughts and emotions. So, the energetic field around them grows. And, as this process continues, this momentum grows and becomes stronger. The energy becomes more attracting.

- Then, providing your attention is on what you desire, and you do not throw a spanner in the works, more ideas will flow to you, and you meet more people who can help you, and something you read sparks off an ah-ha moment, and all the resources you require to realize your desires, just flow to you.

This process of allowing yourself to receive what you desire, unfolds in much the same way that a skier gathers momentum as he moves down the slope. Until, in next to no time, he's sweeping down the mountainside at a terrific rate of knots.

In the face of no-resistance, momentum gathers pace fast and furiously.

Think about it for a moment:

Not so long ago, we were trading baubles for food. We were riding horses, then Model T's, and now Supercars that are clocking speed of 0-200 kph in mid-4's!

We took to the skies, then to the Moon, and now to Mars. From steam trains to bullet trains. From ox-power to nuclear power. From TNT to H-Bombs. From the abacus to algorithmic deep machine learning. And, just where has it all come from?

Have you ever stopped to think where all the things have come from, that continue to expand and evolve our species?

From thoughts turning into things. That's where everything comes from. From vibrational reality turning into physical reality.

Because every creation, each manifestation, no matter how large or small, starts with a vibration that becomes a thought, that gathers feeling, that is then dreamt about. Imagined. Visualized. Focussed into physical Being.

And if you have the ability to think it, the universe most certainly has the ability to deliver it to you.

You see, the process of deliberate creation is much like the process of germination, or gestation. The only difference between these processes, is that you don't get to observe the vibrational process. There are no scopes or scans that offer assurance that the process of becoming, *is* in fact underway. You only see the end result – the physical manifestation.

However, there are any number of clues along the way. You just need to know what to 'look' for, and where to find them. But unless this path of deliberate alignment is your chosen journey, the knowledge is not revealed.

Which is why everyone is not deliberately creating. Because most people want to see it, before they will believe it. Which is the antithesis of intentional creation.

Deliberate creators know that their desires are already vibrational creations. They know that their thoughts have already germinated in the realm of vibration. And that between their Guiding-selves and the law of attraction, these thoughts have gathered all that was necessary for them to become things. They already exist.

Your Guiding-self's pure, positive vibration, has attracted to each of your desires – all those you know, and all those you don't remember – more and more, that will surprise and delight you.

A deliberate creator knows that all (s)he now needs to do, is to focus on that becoming, in a light and sure way.

And as you continue to align with the pure positive energy in which that thought came to you – the pure positive energy that your non-physical partner holds it in, and in which it has expanded – that thought continues to gather momentum, until ... here it is ... that thing you wanted!

More importantly, that thing you never doubted you could have.

Ah, therein lies the rub.

THE DOUBTING

The rub that messes it all up, lies in your doubting.

IN your worry. In your fear. In your not-believing. In all those emotions you experience, that carry a markedly different energetic field to the one that surrounded your idea, when you first received it.

When this brain-child of yours was fresh and new and fine. However, seldom, for long.

You start out eagerly, sure of the veracity of your new idea, of your new desire. And, sure of yourself. And then, often almost immediately, the doubt starts to creep in.

Have I bitten off more than I can chew? Where will the money come from? What if this doesn't work? Who am I, to think I can pull this off?

We stifle ourselves. We bog ourselves down with what-if, what-if, what-if? Sure, we keep moving forward with our idea, but because of our uncertainty, the momentum of its becoming slows down. The impetus starts to shift.

Then you talk to someone whose opinion matters to you. Although it shouldn't. And they say "Are you mad, do you see what's happening out there?". Or, "You can't trust anyone these days". Or, "You don't have the training, or the knowledge'. Or, "it's out of your field". Or, "You're too old", or "too young", or the wrong this, or too that. And fresh doubt creeps in.

Perhaps you're watching a show, and hear similar opinions being expressed. And that gets you thinking. "Wow, maybe they're right." And more doubt sets in. And things slow down even further. Because the energy field around your desire is being eroded by your doubt.

The momentum you initially had going, continues to dissipate. It's if you're simultaneously pressing the up-and-down elevator buttons. Stop-Go-Stop-Go. Can I? Can't I? Can I? Can't I?

Then the meeting you were hoping for, that you considered pivotal, is cancelled. And that other thing you were relying on, fails to materialize. And you say to yourself. "You see, I just knew I was overreaching. Well, at least I tried. But obviously it wasn't meant to be."

What utter poppycock! Not only *was* it meant to be. Your desire has *already* come into vibrational Be-ing. Your wish has already been granted. It is done. It already *is*.

And, in terms of the beautiful, eternal dance of expansion that is swirling around you and your non-physical partner, your Guiding-self is already living that desire.

In other words:

- You delivered your part: Life caused you to ask, and so you did. You vibrated your desire into being.

- Your Guiding-self delivered their part: They held the vibrational essence of your desire. And continue to do so.

- Then the universe gathered together all that was needed, to realize your desire into full vibrational manifestation.

- If you had only remained true to your course. If you had aligned your habitual thoughts to the desire you had birthed. If you had not replaced your early eagerness and sure-footedness with doubt. Then the universe would have led you all the way to your desire. And to the expansion you seek.

You see, when you quieten your mind, you stop thinking resistant thoughts. You stop questioning. You stop doubting. And when the chatter stops, your vibration is free to rise. And it does.

The same effect is achieved, when you're in a happy place. When you're feeling loving, and kind and eager and satisfied and enthusiastic, then your vibration resets to this higher resonance.

And it is in these moments, when you sense the complete stillness of your mind, or you feel joy seeping through your smile and through your Being, that you are in harmony with All that you are.

Then, *you* are feeling the way non-physical you, *always* feels. Then, you are seeing the world through the eyes of your Guiding-self, as it were. And your life looks amazing.

Because you really are meant to have everything you want.

But as we've seen, much of the time, instead of believing this; instead of moving forward with the idea, in the certainty of its already vibrational existence, you allow yourself to listen to everyone else, and to your own second-guessing.

You take your eye off what you want, and replace it with what you see and hear around you. You shift your attention and your musings, to the reality of what is already manifested around you. And the truth of the matter is, that this is all such old news.

What-is, is the culmination of everything that has already been vibrated into Being. What-is, represents all the old desires, and fears and wishes and ideas and doubts. The everything, of all that has ever been.

What-is, is what everyone else, through time, has created. And those who are observing it, are merely adding to it. Merely observing, and expanding it. Nothing new.

Which is the reason that what-is, usually represents the very absence of what you desire. You have chosen what you want. But you have not yet focussed what you want, in the precise way that you want it, into physical Being.

So, as you continue to focus here, on what you observe around you, you find more of what is calibrated to the absence of what you desire.

Without meaning to, and without seeing that you have, you self-fulfil your own prophesy: "Oh well, perhaps I'll have better luck next time". With the caveat, "If there is a next time."

Happily, there always are next times. WellBeing never stops flowing to you. It is your natural state of Being. WellBeing is the natural state of our universe. WellBeing is eternal. Just like you are.

But, if you don't consciously shift yourself up that emotional scale toward it, the flow will continue past you. It doesn't matter how many opportunities come your way; you will remain blinkered to them.

Like ships passing, unseen in the night, you cannot access that which resonates at either a higher vibration, or a lower vibration, than your own resonance, in this moment.

SAVOUR EVERY MORSEL

Along your path of deliberate creation, meditate first. And then, as your day progresses, take time to find things to appreciate.

APPRECIATION is another highly effective way to tune yourself to the higher frequency of the Universal Well-Being, that is yours.

The Well-Being that is flowing to you in every moment. The Well-Being that you just need to allow in.

"Riiight!", you say, "did you happen to see the news this morning? Ha! So, what's there to appreciate?"

Oh, there is *so* much to appreciate. It's boundless. But, from that emotional place of doom-and-gloom:

- It isn't easy to feel appreciation for your body, that breathed all night long without you having to do a thing. And for the unending supply of oxygen supporting you, and all around you.

- You may not be thankful for the magnificence of your planet, that is spinning perfectly in its orbit.

- You're not going to readily appreciate the beauty of the sun that rose this morning, and in which you had absolutely no involvement.

- You are probably not revelling in the fact that you are loved beyond measure.

- You are unlikely to be joyous in the knowledge, that you can create anything you can dream of. And that you have unending help to accomplish its manifestation.

- You almost certainly cannot yet acknowledge, that paying attention to the media, keeps you firmly focussed on all the what-is, that is taking place around you.

Yet, despite all this, you absolutely *can* find some-thing that will make you feel a little better. Any-thing that will lift you from the feelings of vulnerability, or anxiety, or rage, or jealousy, or despair, that have now attached to you, from the things you've been looking at, and listening to.

In every moment, and regardless of what is going on around you, you can *choose how you want to feel*. And you do so by being selective in what you give your attention to.

As with quietening your mind, consciously choosing to feel better, is wholly within your power to achieve. And it really is not that complicated: Make the decision, moment-by-moment, and then line-up with it.

With practise, you will find it becoming easier and easier to shift into that better feeling place. Because you will find yourself looking and listening less and less, to all the things that unsettle you.

Does this mean you're not being pragmatic? That you're not facing reality? Not at all. It means you're being selectively discerning. You are actively choosing what to allow into your experience, rather than passively accepting everything you are exposed to.

Deliberate creation means acknowledging the existence of two re-alities:

- A physical reality, that you can observe. And hear and taste and smell and touch.

- A vibrational reality, that you can experience through your thoughts and feelings.

And, just as you choose what you manifest into your vibrational reality, you get to choose what you manifest in your physical reality. The choice is:

- "Do I focus indiscriminately on what-is, and allow it all in?", or

- "Do I allow into my experience only that which uplifts me?"

You see, feeling good does *not need to be conditional* upon what is happening in your life, nor on what is going on around you.

In fact, feeling good cannot be tethered to conditions.

Unfortunately, however, this is how you perceive it to be, much of the time.

- You hold the practised thought pattern that: *If* this happens, *then* I'll feel this way.

- When the truth of the matter is: By *feeling* this way, *then* this will happen.

How you feel should *never* be conditional upon what is playing out around you. Nor should you feeling better, *ever* be conditional upon what others do. Or, more often than not – on what they are not doing.

However, the manifestation, or the non-manifestation, of everything you experience, or don't experience, is always conditional upon how you feel.

As long as you need something to happen, in order to feel better; as long as your happiness is reliant upon something happening, you remain powerless to create the life you desire. Because calibrating yourself to conditions, implies that you are reliant on other people. And, as we know, other people can be fickle.

Oh, they don't mean to be. And neither do you. But once you accept that each and every person on our planet is motivated by the desire to feel better, how can you possibly expect to improve your vibration, when you hand over the on-off toggle to someone else? Who is also only wanting to feel better?

They, too, are searching for objects, and people, and events to make them feel better than they are feeling now. So, while you may feel good for the period you hold each other in positive focus, looking for your joy outside of yourself is simply not sustainable.

Right now, you may be feeling great. But later today, your significant other, or your colleague, or your child, or that stranger you meet, may be feeling off, and your interaction leaves you feeling slighted.

And 'wap', there goes your good-feeling energy, as you find yourself sliding down the emotional scale. Whereafter, you need to begin the upward shift all over again. And all over again, the next time something similar happens, as it will. And again.

Far rather, you take back control of your vibrational toggle. Find the stability that comes from learning to be unconditional.

Rather than thinking: "I'll feel this way, if this happens", start practising: "I choose to feel this way now. And now. And now. Irrespective of what happens, or what is happening."

Does this sound too difficult? It really needn't be. Because you already have the tools you need to achieve unconditional vibrational stability. And you get to that place by:

- o   Identifying what you're feeling.

- o   Being aware of the 'why' of it. Not analyzing the why of it. Not delving into the why of your feelings about it. Nor the 'when', nor 'how'.

- o   Recognizing that paying attention to it, is not feeling good.

- o   Then 'looking' away.

You see, you have another perfectly crafted tool to help you along your path of deliberate creation. This is your elaborate system of emotions.

- o   Your emotions are really an intricate guidance system, that signals to you, moment-by-moment, precisely where your energetic footprint is.

- o   Like a finely honed GPS, your emotions provide the ideal way to cue you, to adjust your focus.

- o   All you ever need to do, is to tap in to how you are feeling. And let your emotions show you the way.

When you focus on a subject that causes you negative feeling, your emotions let you know straight away. Then you can choose to stay there. Or you can choose to intentionally shift your attention away from that subject. Towards some-thing, or those things, you really like thinking about, because they really leave you feeling good every time you think about them.

As you do so, and that pleasant feeling starts rising within you, stay with it for as long as you can. You may feel the pleasure of it in the region of your solar plexus, or around your heart, in your chest. You may spontaneously break into a grin. In whichever way you experience this positive feeling, savour every morsel of it.

Play the event, or the happening, over and again in your mind. Visualize it in detail. How it feels. How it looks. The satisfying, pleasing outcome. Try to involve more of your senses. See if you can smell that fragrance, or feel the cuddliness, or the bracing chill, or hear the love in the vibration of it.

Doesn't matter if it was a time then, a time now, or a time yet to come; past, present, or future. Just find a subject to focus your mind on, that makes you feel better than you do, in your present state of doom-and-gloom.

Then, as your pleasure in the remembering of it, and in the visualisation of it grows, be conscious of your shift into a better-feeling space.

If you are conjuring a new image of a desire not yet manifested, let it feel to you as real as if it has already occurred. It will become a new memory.

Whilst you savour these lovely thoughts, don't get into the specifics of them. These will often bog you down, and whisk you straight out of your pleasure zone. Just paint your pleasure in the imagining of them, with broad brush strokes.

In your savouring, more thoughts that feel better will flow to you. And, in this way, the momentum around this new better-feeling will continue to expand.

Abraham[4] teaches that just 17 seconds of singular thought, is sufficient time to activate another thought of an equivalent vibration. And, that after just 68 seconds of continued focus, the power of the momentum gathered, causes a shift into an entirely new vibration.

The moment I heard this, my spirits soared at the knowledge, which was a sure-fire sign as to its truth.

But, remember that this works both ways: The Universe does not differentiate between the vibration of the thoughts and feelings

---

[4] Abraham is the name selected by a non-physical group consciousness, a part of Source energy, that is received and translated by internationally renowned, Esther Hicks.

you are choosing, and experiencing. So, if you focus where you don't want to be, the law of attraction will take you there just as quickly.[5]

◆◆◆◆◆◆

Now, back to that place of positive thoughts and feelings, that you are *expanding through your focus*. That is the aim.

Why do you want to savour every positive morsel?

- Because it feels increasingly good. And that's precisely how you want to feel, more of the time.

- Because, with both time and practise, you will become so adept at finding that feeling, you won't necessarily need a particular subject to get you thinking and feeling that way.

- You'll be able to do so, with just a single word. Like flicking a switch: 'Happy, or 'content', or 'eager'. And 'click', "Yes, I am".

- Because this is how you teach yourself to manage your own energetic emanations. It's how you become an unconditional creator.

As you extend the time you spend in feeling good, there will come the moment when you'll find yourself able to stand solidly in this higher, finer vibration, no matter what is going on around you.

---

[5] Tongue in cheek, then I guess if you *do* feel the need to think about, or share something of a less than desirable nature, you need to talk fast. And do so, in less than 17 seconds!

That's mastery. And that's ultimately where you want to be.

Because when you imagine anything with genuine feeling and intent, your mind will, before long, start believing it to be true.

You see, your mind does not differentiate between your physical- and your vibrational realities. So, the longer you stay with those high-flying memories, thoughts, and visualizations, the greater the energy field that you'll build around them.

And when you do, you'll benefit from a whole different outlook.

Then, take this new outlook, this new improved energetic footprint, out into the world with you, and see what an improved response you receive from all around you.

If it doesn't happen this time, practise it again tomorrow and tomorrow and tomorrow. With practise, your vibrational shift will come. And with it, the shift in your life experience will happen.

It *must* come. It's universal law.

AIRTIME COMES AT A PRICE

Creating is about vibration. And about attraction. And then there's the all-important component of allowing that which you want, into your experience.

BACK to the importance of the awareness of your thoughts: When you become aware of what you're thinking, you can then begin to consciously think, the way you want to think, in order to *feel*, the way you want to feel. And we know we are all reaching toward feeling better in the moment.

Said differently: By becoming a conscious thinker, you can replace a previously practiced way of thinking, with a different modality. Hence, you can change the way you predominantly feel. You can master your vibration.

What complicates the simplicity of this, is that all-pervasive attraction. Because, if you are accustomed to a certain way of thinking, the fast-moving energy field around these habits of thought, built up over time, make it a tad more difficult, but not impossible, to shift.

So again: If you recognize a pattern of thought that does not serve you well, and you set the intention to replace it, you need to be patient with yourself. Afterall, a belief is nothing more than a practised thought. A thought that you keep thinking.

Yes, it is practiced. Yet, it is also *temporary*.

So, if you replace it with a different thought, pretty soon you won't be thinking that old thought anymore. If you don't give it airtime, it will simply cease to be.

Providing, you don't try to get to the bottom of: "Why am I thinking this way?", and "When, did I start thinking this way? And "How can I change this thought?" No. Leave it alone. No sifting and sorting and analyzing. Drop it right where it is. Give it no more airtime.

It doesn't matter how, or why, or when you started thinking this way.

What matters is that you:

- Identify the way you're thinking.

- Consciously elect to replace what you're thinking about, with another thought that has you feeling better.

- Actively do so. Start thinking differently to the way you were.

- Period.

This applies across the board. Which is the reason for you wanting to give airtime only to that which you feel better about, when thinking about.

As you practise this, moment by moment, day by day, your mood will begin to improve. And with it, your life will begin to improve, as the universe starts yielding to you, more of what you want.

"Practice?", you ask.

o Yes. Because that's what you've been doing your whole life. You're a practised thinker.

o You may just not yet have realized it. Realized that every thought that you've ever thought, has brought you right to this moment. And, that despite what you may be feeling, it really is all just fine.

o   Because, in case you didn't know it: *Everything* is *always* working out for you.

So, if, for the most part, you are filled with a passion for life, then keep on thinking those happy thoughts that you have been thinking. And you'll keep receiving more of the same, as you continue to live the joyous life you intended.

However, if there is an area of your life that is troubling you, that too, is clear evidence of the vibrational nature of your thoughts on that subject.

It is evidence of you either having:

•   Practised yourself into a habit of doubt, or

•   Practised yourself into being objective.

You probably rather pride yourself on being objective. On your examining both sides of the coin. On examining the pros and cons of the situation.

But what you may not have known, is that usually after examining the pros and cons of your thought or idea, you then split your focus between that which you are experiencing, and that which you want to experience.

In so doing, you dissipate your creative power. And you do this, much of the time.

◆ ◆ ◆ ◆ ◆ ◆

Let us explore in a little more detail:

Perhaps one of your relationships is troubling. Or your job is unsatisfying. Or you want more money. Or you feel stuck. In essence: You want some-thing that you have not yet got.

Now we know that in every situation, the underlying premise to success – meaning, happiness – is for you to:

o   Stop paying attention to what you don't want, in this already manifested reality.

o   Start paying attention to what you do want, in your vibrational reality.

"But, how?", you ask, "can I possibly stop paying attention to everything that is going on around me? It's right here. All around me. I can see it; I can hear it. I can talk about it with others."

Yes, indeed: What-is, is all about you, all the time.

But, consider this:

Assume you're seated in a restaurant and perusing the menu. Are your eyes immediately drawn to the items that are not appealing to you? Or do your eyes skim over those items that you've decided, through your life experience, you do not like, and come to rest on those dishes that tantalise your palate?

The latter, for sure. Because usually, you afford as little air-time as possible, to that which you do *not* want to include in your taste experience.

In making your selection, you then engage your senses further. You may conjure a mental picture of the dish, or imagine what it will taste like. Or, perhaps you cast your mind back. And recall: what it tasted like, a time previously, or, the wonderful evening you enjoyed when you ordered a similar dish.

You effortlessly analyze the data, and you choose. And, you generally don't choose the thing you don't want. Although often, you *do* allow your choice to be dictated by the interests of others. By the what-is, that is around you.

For instance:

Are the ingredients fattening, or non-fattening, as per the latest fad I've been following? Is this meal wholesome or unhealthy, as per the latest medical opinions I've read about? Does my menu selection offer value for money, or am I being over-charged, as per the opinion of my close friend? Is this what I really want to order, or is it what my budget dictates, as per my glaring bank balance? Am I wanting to impress, or I can relax and be me, as per my practised thoughts?

In the moment, a myriad factors can affect our decision-making. And yet, you make that menu choice in next to no time. And then you sit back, and engage with those at your table, whilst looking forward to receiving your meal.

You also do not place your order, expecting it to be served it to you immediately. You know it will take some time to prepare; that unseen hands in the kitchen need to gather together the ingredients for the specific meal you have selected, and combine them in delicious ways to please you.

In the act of choosing what you wanted, you initiated a process that you trust in. And you are prepared to wait, in the certainty that the manifestation of your desire is on its way to you. And that you need do nothing more, to ensure its arrival.

Is this ringing any bells for you?

In the same way, when your car needs attention, you take it to the dealership in the expectation of it being repaired. You don't demand to go into the workshop to oversee what the mechanic will do. You expect your desire to meet. And your car to be returned to you, in tip-top shape.

You choose, and you birth new desires all day long. And then, you wait. In positive expectation that things will work out for you, just the way you want them to.

In the interim, you get on with other things. You don't spend your day fretting about your car. You don't call the workshop every few hours to check on progress. You relax into the process with certainty. And turn your attention to other matters.

So, why then, when it comes to anything more than the genre of your day-to-day desires, that you positively expect to be met, do the wheels fall off?

Because the things that you really, really want, are usually the things that you:

- Hold to be important, and therefore not readily available;

- Feel are great in magnitude, and hence difficult to attain;

- Consider to be rare, and so in limited supply;

- Imagine are in some way special, and reserved for those who are special;

- Believe that you, of all people, do not deserve, or are not worthy of.

In addition, these are also the subjects that you spend most time thinking about. And worrying about. And wondering about. And noting the absence of. And building a Whippet-speed, powerful vibration of doubt around.

In other words, these are the very subjects that you are not allowing yourself to receive.

Yet there really is no need for you to keep doing so. Afterall, we know that it is entirely within your ability to choose what you give your attention to. You get to decide what movie you keep playing in your mind.

So then, isn't it logical to just start choosing discerningly where you place your attention?

Let us take a look at how this could unfold:

Should you wish for a better relationship – whether with your spouse, partner, child, parent, business associate, colleague, supplier, client, neighbour:

- Identify the qualities in the other that you like. And focus upon them. And only upon them. Do this when you are in contact with each other, and whenever your thoughts turn to this person.

- Stay away from your practised thinking about those attributes that get you mad, bad, sad, or frustrated. Do not cogitate upon anything you believe they have done that has upset you.

Pay attention solely to the attributes that you enjoy, and sooner or later that person will begin to offer you only those attributes.

You see, you always get what you expect.

And attributes carry an energetic footprint, too. So, if you train yourself into the uptight vibration of someone, that is all that attraction will continue to bring to you.

Focus on, talk about, push against, expect, their grumpy or unhelpful bits, and the law of attraction will bring you more of that. Pay attention to, and expect their happy helpful bits, and attraction will bring to you more that share these finer energetic footprints. Not just from this one, but from all the others, too.

Until then, if their helpful happy bits are in short supply, don't try digging for them. Rather reach for those better feeling thoughts that you always find, on that totally different subject.

Similarly, should you want more money:

- Practise yourself into a feeling of the richness of your current life experience. Not your vibrational financial abundance, because *that* you probably have doubts about. So, stay away from the subject of money altogether.

- Rather acknowledge your abundance in your vitality; in your Wellbeing. Find your prosperity in the bounty of nature that provides for you, never-endingly; and in the perfection of your planet. Feel your wealth in the multitude of things you enjoy each day, that go largely unnoticed.

- As you continue to practice, and to keep your attention from your bank balance, start noticing the evidence of your abundance in: The thoughtfulness of a stranger; the delicious aroma of your coffee; the smile you receive; the invitation to jump the queue; the song that plays on the radio just as you think of it.

- These are manifestations, too. Notice them. These manifestations of the abundance that your improved vibration is attracting.

Then, a shift *will* come in your financial position. Because abundant is abundant. There are no half measures, here. And when you truly feel abundant, even if only in one area of your life, attraction will parlay this into abundance across all areas of your life.

◆◆◆◆◆◆

Through it all, be easy on yourself. When something happens, that you'd prefer didn't happen to you, don't go beating yourself up, as in: "I should have known better", or "I should have done it differently", or "I'm such an idiot", or "will I never learn?"

No! Be kind to yourself. Be generous with yourself. Afterall, you know it is only attraction. Remind yourself that: "Nothing's gone wrong. On the contrary, *my emotions are my guidance system.*"

"And this unpleasant feeling is telling me that, right now, my Guiding-self does not feel about this thing, or this person, or this experience, in the same way that I do. And that's why I'm feeling lousy".

Then, take a few deep breaths, thank the universe for their guidance, and start again tomorrow ... and tomorrow ... and tomorrow.

You see, being in alignment with your Guiding-self, is not like a race you run. And for which you are then awarded a medal, as evidence of your achievement. Nor is your improved vibration akin to a degree you successfully study for. And then receive a certificate to hang on your wall.

Aligning with your non-physical partner happens in this moment, and in this moment. And in the next. Moment-to-moment.

Raising your vibration happens forever in the 'now'.

And because your improved vibration is a dynamic state of Being, as you live your life and shift your gaze from what has already been created physically, to what you have created vibrationally, you're bound to have mixed emotions at times. And that's just fine.

In fact, you *must* have mixed emotions at times. Your desire for expansion ensures that you will.

Because *in* that space, the process starts over. As intended:

You will again exercise your choice about what you don't want, and what you do. And the pure desire that emanates from you will again be focussed upon, with singular intentionality, by your

Guiding-self. And this non-physical part of you will become, will experience, your vibrational desire.

And the Law of Attraction will add to it. And so, the universe will gather together all that is needed for you to bring your desire into physical manifestation. And the non-physical part of you will set about guiding you, by dropping ideas and impulses into your mind, and prompting you to the rendezvous, and to the people necessary for its full manifestation.

All you have to do. The *only* thing you have to do .... Is to stay happily focussed on your desire. And to reach for better feeling thoughts during your daily experiences.

You also have to be aware not to allow doubt, or the opinions of others, to start you pressing, simultaneously, those up-and-down elevator buttons.

Because if you do, that elevator will never gain the momentum necessary to take you where you want to Be. Stop-Go-Stop-Go-Stop-Go.

That's all!

Believe it. Expect it. And, sooner than later, it will be. That's universal law.

IT'S ALL IN THE WAVE

You came into physical Being with the tools you need to translate vibration. These attributes are your five senses.

QUANTUM physics tells us that most of what-is, is not. That most of what-is, is seeming emptiness. Or mis-leading emptiness, whichever view you adopt.

Yet, humanity has no hesitation at all in believing in this so-called physical reality. Despite that everything that we perceive as being physically manifested, is barely 0,0000001% here.

So, when you sit on a chair, or lie on your bed, you're actually hovering above it, physicists tell us. And that has to do with electron 'swarms', and electron displacement and ... guess what? .... Energy[6]!

This being the case, how then does one see or hear or smell or taste or touch, that which is 99,9% not here?

You do so, courtesy of your senses. That are expert translators of vibration.

---

[6] Do you get the connection? Energy ... vibration ... vibrational reality. It's not that these concepts are 'out there'. They are right here.

When you see something, you do so because your eyes are able to identify an energetic form, and translate it into a material form.

When you hear something, your ears are translating an energetic movement, a pulsating resonance, into sound.

Reminds me of the oft posed question – If a tree falls in a forest and there's no-one there to hear it, does it make a sound? The answer is a resounding 'Yes'. Because in forests, there is always life of sensory form. So, in the absence of human presence, a falling tree will always be heard.

When you detect a scent, an aroma, or an odour, you do so through your olfactory senses, that are, in effect, translating *that* vibration. Those energetic wave-lengths. Although there is also usually an expectation of an aroma from the visual cue.

Which is the reason for you anticipating a sweet fragrance, when you see a pretty flower. And the reason why a Rose that has no fragrance can be disappointing. Because when you see its beauty, you expect it to smell delicious, too.

When it doesn't, your expectation is not met, which begs the question. 'When I saw the rose, did I expect a fragrant scent, or did I wonder if it had a sweet fragrance? What was I giving energy to?

In other words, was it my uncertainty, my doubting, that resulted in my not detecting, and not translating the scent that was there?'

Back to the translation of matter:

If perception implies identification through your senses, and it does. Then it also means that which you perceive, along the chain of creating, becomes some-thing.

Said differently: Your perceptions create matter.

In the same way, you also create through the power of your mind. Not through a process of will-power, nor mental effort. Not by trying to ignore what-is, and convince yourself otherwise. But through the power of your magnificent, boundless imagination.

As we said earlier, your mind does not differentiate between that which is physically manifested, and that which is vibrationally created. Which means that when you deliberately focus on a subject, or topic, your mind accepts the general reality of it. And in accepting the reality of it, brings you closer to the attainment of it.

Moreover, when you focus you mind into its imagining mode, you also activate your senses. So, when you do this with intention, after meditation or after appreciation – when you have arrested resistant thought, or are in a place of Well-Being – you powerfully engage all your tools in aligning with the 'Whole' of who you are, that brings you closer to your desires.

Perhaps, Sir Charles Lyell's phrase 'mind over matter', may be well suited for use in this context: Mind first. Matter second.

And, in this way, this ethos, this awareness of the art of deliberate creating, the art of aligning, the art of vibrational translation, need never become bound up in spiritual debate.

The Creator-Force, God, the 'I Am that I Am', *is*. Everywhere. Both within and without. As above, so below. Similarly, the authenticity of our personal, as it were, Guiding-self, is a given. Regardless of the myriad different names describing this – Intuition, Spirit, Soul, Higher self, Angel, Inner Being.

All is One. And One is All.

The debate need not be evoked, because the fundamental tools of conscious creating, in these physical bodies, comprise your thoughts, your emotions, your senses and your mind. And each of these tools is known to you, and is familiar to you. Although understood only in part.

In other words:

- o   Your senses translate vibrations into things you see, hear, smell, taste, and touch.

- o   Your emotions translate vibrations into things you feel; into feelings.

- o   Your mind translates vibrations into both thoughts and images.

Therefore: If you believe it, you can visualize it.

And if you can visualize it, your mind can translate the vibration of those images, and of those thoughts, all thoughts, into some-thing. Into everything that you experience.

Said differently: You *have* to believe it, in order to see it, which is where the beliefs that you hold, come into the mix.

We could in fact say: The art of creating is really *the art of translating vibration into matter*:

Which means that key to your deliberate creating, is your ability to direct your attention to translating vibrations into matter you want. Rather than indiscriminately translating whatever vibrations are available to you.

Because when you indiscriminately translate vibrations, you attract to yourself a mixed bag of that which you want, together with that which you'd definitely rather not have.

This effectively backs into what we have previously explored, albeit from a different approach.

And it is this mixed-bag variety, that most people are preoccupied with.

YOU CREATE WITH EASE

By way of an analogy, let us consider the lives that have been, and continue to be, created by two uncles: Edgar and Darly.

IN his latter years, an unwanted life change resulted in uncle Edgar relocating to a part of the country he came to dislike for the weather. He will tell you how much, during any conversation.

He could have moved, but feels he cannot. And, over time uncle Edgar has come to dislike not only the climate, but the people living there, too. Their attitudes. Their behaviour. Even the way they drive.

"They are simply not my kind of people", he'll remark. And, certainly, based on his earlier life experience, many are indeed different.

Yet, there are those who *are* his kind of people. He just does not perceive it this way. He has made up his mind that this is not true, and so, he prefers not to socialize.

Some time back, uncle Edgar developed an unidentifiable pain in his foot. The severity varies from acute to 'not too bad', for no apparent reason. And, whereas he used to enjoy long, leisurely walks, he now no longer seems keen on even taking short strolls.

He is venturing out less, and so his daily experience is contracting. Particularly now, as his ability to drive with ease, is also being affected.

And this entire cycle of events, is all as a result of the manifestation of a problematic foot.

Such is the power of his mind over the matter he is creating. The matter that is not what he wants, but *is* where his focus lies, and so matters to him.

Now, one may reasonably assume that uncle Edgar is not intentionally creating a smaller life for himself. Nor could he possibly want a painful foot. Certainly not. Afterall, his foot was not always painful. Then one day, it was. And a little more so, as time progressed.

We're not suggesting he awoke one morning and decided he wanted a sore foot. But he did awake one morning feeling unhappy. And then on a following morning he didn't like the weather. Sometime after that, he found the people he was encountering on a daily basis, were not to his liking, either. And then his driving experience became unpleasant, due to "all the idiots on the road".

Little wonder then, that as he has become more disillusioned with his environment, the painful foot is increasingly keeping him from venturing into this world around him.

Now that uncle Edgar is spending more time in his home, his immediate surroundings are starting to become an irritant: Too many heavy books. Photographs that are too great in number. Dust that turns his computer from grey to brown, and "the darn thing doesn't work properly, anyway." Even the sun gets its share of blame, as it is too harsh and scorches the plants on his patio.

This unhappy, disgruntled mind, that for some years has been finding fault with much in his outer world, has now turned its attention to his inner sanctum. So, when uncle Edgar recently also developed a problem with his balance, we were not really surprised at another physical manifestation of things going awry.

In a sense, it really is a work of art. Because, here to see in life-size actualization, are the physical creations of his perceptions. The manifestations of his mind.

As uncle Edgar's translation of what he sees has become cloaked in negativity, the experiences he is manifesting have increasingly grown into what he does not desire. Because the momentum around these negative feelings has become so powerful, so undeniable, that it has become his dominant vibration.

His life has become a case of the self-fulfilling prophesy of: "See, I told you so!"

Now, uncle Darly's latter life experience was also marked by difficult change.

He, too, has a strong disposition and a dispersed family. And he also needed to relocate unexpectedly, at a time when he reasonably expected his life to be sweet. Even more to the point, is that he literally needed to start over financially.

Today he manages his own small business, interacts with others discerningly, and appreciates his surroundings. He has also grown closer to his family, from whom he was estranged.

Uncle Darly is not readily judgemental, meditates regularly, and so, it's not surprising that he tends to find his glass half full, more often than half empty.

Through his perceptions, and mental constructs, uncle Darly has created a more positive life experience for himself. Rather than praying for things to be better, he gives thanks for each day that is.

Both uncles have been, and remain, unconscious creators of their worlds. Yet they have been busily creating two very different lives: The shrinking life experience created through the disillusionment of the one, contrasts sharply with the happier, healthier life experience created through the general optimism of the other.

Now, if we add to this potent mix of perception and mind-power creation, an acceptance and understanding of the laws of the universe, an exciting potentiality emerges.

FEEL BETTER, GET BETTER

Like the law of gravity, the Law of Attraction operates with perfect, and absolute, consistency.

AND, in the example of the two uncles, the power of the attraction of like to like, is clearly evident. In the creation of their dominant vibrations, through their focus, they have manifested all that they are living.

This is not to say that uncle Edgar has not enjoyed many successes, rewarding times and joyful experiences. Nor that uncle Darly has not felt angry, sad, and down-in-the-dumps at times.

Their lives are a well-mixed bag. Because like most, they have been creating by default rather than with intent.

And as is always the case, the lives they are living represent what they focus on, what they talk about, what they observe, how they feel, the nature of their expectations, their beliefs, their outlooks.

But what if uncle Edgar had, at some point come across the concept of attraction. And in a moment of inspiration, he'd seized upon the opportunity to consciously actuate in his experience, the premise of 'like to like is drawn'.

What might this scenario look like?

He's tripping along merrily, and then something happens to change his mood. Perhaps he experiences a brusque encounter with a stranger.

- Best case scenario: Because he cares about feeling good, uncle Edgar is generally tuned-in to how he is feeling.

  o As a result, he registers moving out of his previously held place of good feeling, and into one of anger or irritation.

  o This early awareness halts the shift in the direction of the new emotion, as he consciously moves his focus away from the encounter, and reaches for a subject that feels better.

  o In doing so, attraction would not gain meaningful traction.

  o Consequently, it will be easy for uncle Edgar to re-create the positive emotional environment he was previously enjoying.

- Second scenario: Uncle Edgar fails to acknowledge his emotional shift in the early stages.

  o Consequently, he provides fertile ground for attracting another thought of a similar lower vibration.

  o Now, not only is he feeling offended by that individual's brusque manner, but he is also reminded of the driver who cut him off earlier in the week. And that felt pretty uncomfortable, and was downright unfair.

  o After just 17 seconds of these two thoughts banging around together, uncle Edgar might recall someone closer, who also tended to be brusque in their interactions. And that didn't feel good either.

  o As the attraction of similar resonating thoughts continues, after just 68 seconds he would shift into this new energetic place of feeling lousy.

This is not to say that uncle Edgar would not again be able to think-feel his way out of this new unpleasant vibration, that he would prefer not to be experiencing. He would be able to.

But, due to the momentum already gathered, and continuing to gather, his emotional shift would require more focus.

He would need to find another way of Being, in that moment. He would need to walk away. Excuse himself if necessary. And break the momentum through conscious distraction.

For instance:

- o   Finding something pleasing to do;

- o   Making a list of things to appreciate;

- o   Taking a nap;

- o   Meditating – although it would be difficult to quieten the mind under these conditions, when it's attracting a rampage of thoughts.

If music were uncle Edgar's passion, and as he is out-and-about at this time, the easiest could be to distract himself with a favourite tune. Or to imagine himself in his favourite theatre, enjoying a production of his favourite show.

There is no magic formula here. You need to figure out what works best for you. Also knowing that what works in this moment, may not necessarily work next time. But with practice, and patience, you will get a handle on what works for you, soon enough.

- Third scenario: Uncle Edgar did not catch his emotional shift at all, and the momentum really got rolling.

  - o   His thoughts are now running rampant. And he has no option but to roll with it. To let his upsetting emotions run their course, as they surely will.

When you experience this, do *not* berate yourself for not catching your emotional shift early enough. Because your Guiding-self will certainly not be going down that route.

Your Guiding-self will never, ever follow you down that, or any other dark rabbit-hole you construct. And, if *you* go there, it will only make you feel worse. As you shift further down the vibrational scale. And further away from the 'Whole' of who you are.

Rather appreciate the greater understanding you now have. Then try again tomorrow. And tomorrow. And tomorrow.

You see, nothing's gone wrong. Nothing needs fixing. You have simply had another opportunity to practise your vibrational stability. And we know, that nothing reinforces knowing what you want, like knowing what you don't want.

Even then, when it comes to experiencing the powerful momentum around fear, rooted in years of repetitive triggering, know that it's really tough to shift in the moment. Not impossible, but initially tough.

Afterall, it took years of habitual thinking to set it up. So, it's surely going to take well-practised new thought-patterns to set it down.

So, don't judge yourself, and don't become despondent. Just keep practising your awareness of how you feel in the moment. And keep holding the intention to always reach for a better feeling thought.

Your power lies in every 'Now" moment. It does not matter what you did last year; what happened last month; or even one minute ago. All the counts, is the power that you hold right now. And the tools you have to use that power, right now. And right now.

Know that you *will* reach a point where, if your thoughts go down a particularly well-trodden path, a warning bell of recognition will sound, as you feel your mood change.

This awareness of the change in how you feel, is your Emotional Guidance System at work. Your purposefully-crafted emotional guidance system, that alerts you to choose in every moment. To choose to either continue to feel miserable, or to reach for thoughts that feel better.

I am reminded that when Desk Top Publishing became popular in the '80's, Aldus PageMaker was the software tool widely used. And there was an acronym coined to describe this revolutionary new endeavour – 'WYSIWYG'. Pronounced 'wizzy-wig': What You See Is What You Get. And back then, it really was an accurate description.

Well, this could be said of your life experience, too.

What You See Is What You Get.

In other words: What you focus on, what you give attention to, what you think about, what you talk about, is all and only what you ever get.

So, it's quite logical, really: If you want to 'get better', start paying attention to that which makes you 'feel better'.

Be deliberate in what you focus on. Be discerning and choose wisely. Don't look at things that upset you. Don't listen to things that upset you. Don't talk about things that upset you

Afterall, you generally don't eat or smell things you find unpleasant. So, why not practice the same discernment in what you look at and listen to, all around you?

Because when you do start paying conscious attention to what you allow yourself to see and hear and taste and smell and touch, you become aware of what you are thinking about.

And when you are aware of what you're thinking about, you start noticing how you feel.

And as you start noticing how you feel, you can exercise your choice to only feel better.

And *that's* when you embark on your journey to fulfil your intention of being the intentional creator you were born to be.

Then, the real fun begins.

WHAT DO YOU BELIEVE?

I used to have a saying. It was born from a set of beliefs I held. That I no longer hold to be true.

A T the time, I was unaware of the profound consequences bound up within a set of beliefs. Bound up within the beliefs I previously held, and those I hold now.

Consequences intertwined in the beliefs you hold. Wreathed within every belief ever held by anyone. Because your beliefs underscore your habits of thought.

This means that your beliefs:

- Are the bed-rock of your thinking;

- Determine the actions you take.

And the profundity of this, is that:

- Some of the beliefs you hold, serve you. Whilst others do not.

Yet you chart your way through life largely oblivious to this. With scant regard to the way your beliefs direct both your thinking, and what you do. And, as long as you continue to allow this to be the case, deliberate creating becomes an onerous task, rather than the joyful art of expansion that it is.

Because:

- Your beliefs determine what you allow yourself to receive, and what you keep out.

- When you don't believe that you deserve love, or abundance, or success, or clarity, or security, or joy, or happily, ever after. Then, without even being aware of what you are doing, you keep the up-and-down elevator buttons activated.

  This means giving energy to what you want. Building a little momentum in this direction that you want to move in. Then giving a little energy to what you don't want. Building momentum going in that direction. A little this way. A little that way. Can you see how difficult it then becomes to make any real headway at all?

If something you want remains elusive, you want to examine your beliefs around the likelihood, and the ease, of you receiving this item or event. Do you really and truly believe that you deserve to receive it, and that you can receive it?

In other words: How do you know if a belief you hold is serving you well, or not?

There are always clues along your path. But, if you don't know what to look for, how can you identify them?

You can always tell how your beliefs are serving you, by:

- What is coming to you. In other words, what you are experiencing, and;

- How you feel.

You're bound to see how this plays out, as we take a look at that saying I held to be true. The one I believed in. It went like this:

"We don't learn when things are going smoothly. We learn when things are difficult. And I can overcome these challenges, because I know God never gives us more than we can handle."

This is the explanation I would seek refuge in when things got tough. It somehow justified what I was experiencing. Made the suffering more palatable.

Moreover, a latent spin-off, was that my ability to weather the storm also seemed to garner approval. The more I struggled, the more adjectives like 'capable' and 'strong' and 'amazing' were used.

Yes, no matter how battered and bruised, I always did bounce back from whatever storm was raging at the time: Loss, death, physical challenge, deception, law suits, betrayal, theft, manipulation. And, of course, financial struggle.

Each time, I felt blessed in overcoming the stacked odds. Afterall, was it not proof of having achieved yet another milestone in my growth? But, of course.

And, was it not evidence of my worthiness?

Ouch! I never considered it at the time, but yes, somehow, I had come to equate succeeding in the face of adversity, with evidence of my worthiness.

But why these challenges came to me in the first place remained a mystery. Barring my acceptance that they offered valuable lessons. Although over time, even having seemingly identified the lessons, dissatisfaction in having endured the experience remained. And eventually I began to question the soundness of it all.

Then dawned the acknowledgment, that ever present and underpinning these events, lay the belief that – Challenges in life are opportunities that bring lessons; that in learning the lesson, the challenge is overcome; and that one should feel proud to grow through these challenges. And, this belief extended beyond self, to include everyone.

With this acknowledgment came the realization that, on so many levels, this way of thinking did *not* serve me well.

This belief, meaning this practised way of thinking, did not serve me well. Because:

- Even reading it here feels uncomfortable. And I know for sure this means the vibration of it is nowhere near the vibration of my Guiding-self. And that means it's nowhere near where I want to be.

- When life becomes challenging in a way that the joy gets squeezed out, then something is mightily wrong.

- My very focus on overcoming the challenges that I believed were rightful tests to prove my worth, brought to me those very same challenges. The Law of Attraction saw to that. Now didn't it, just!

Interestingly, on the other end of the stick, another belief seemed to ensure a sort of temperance.

I have always enjoyed a sense of being guided. A feeling that: "The universe has my back".

I unequivocally knew this to be true. And that: "one way or another, things always work out for me" [7].

Now, the nature of this belief, the energy it carries, is altogether different to that of the previous belief in the need to overcome

---

[7] The 'one way or another' evidences doubt in this second part of the belief. A touch of the fingers on the up-and-down elevator buttons.

Now it's cleaned up, and my knowing is crystal clear: Everything is always working out for me. Just as 'everything is always working out for you', too.

challenges. The energetic footprint of this second belief relieves, uplifts, and replenishes.

Despite my faith having been repeatedly and sorely challenged, I have absolutely no doubt that believing the universe always has my back, believing that things always work out for me, has been my saving grace.

Even as these words resonate here, can you feel the vibration – the warmth, the lightness, the sense of coming home?

The vibration around *knowing that someone out here has your back*, lies on a totally different spectrum to the vibration of: 'we are meant to struggle, we are meant to overcome hardship'.

You see, your words and thoughts are vibrational Beings. Their vibrations carry not only meaning, but feeling. In their very utterance, these vibrations have an effect on you. And all around you.

As you realize that words and thoughts powerfully set the tone in all situations. As you start to recognize the strength of the emotional indicators that lie within their resonance. Then you will be able to assess the vibration of your own words, and hence of your own beliefs.

In the feeling of them, you will be able to determine which beliefs are serving you well. Those that make you feel uncomfortable in any way whatsoever, are those habits of thought that are not serving you well. It is these, that you will gain benefit from, in replacing.

THIS MATTERS

An understanding of Who we really are, and why we come to this place we call Earth, has long been impeded by both language and translation.

FOR eons, the language surrounding most teachings of any beneficial nature – has been cloaked in mystery and complexity. And often that which made its way through time, has been greatly altered. And adapted. And edited. And pieced together.

This is true even in our more recent history with regards any mention of the Universal Laws, and vibration.

My breakthrough came with Abraham, and Esther's succinct translating. This was when critical pieces of the extensive jigsaw-puzzle I had been creating, started slotting into place. And together with this, my 'coming of age' in an understanding of the laws of the universe, and the intimate relationship we each share with them.

The way we acquire our beliefs, evolves largely from that which our well-meaning parents, and elders, hold to be true.

They believe something, and we see and hear them living it. And it does seem to be so. Therefore, the logical next step is that we, in turn, accept what our parents believe, to be true. And, in this way the habit of thought is passed along. One generation to the next.

If only, as wise and knowing children, we could choose to accept only those inheritances we know to serve us, and reject those we know do not. Ah, but then again, this too, is part of our expansion.

For instance, I clearly recall my dad saying: "Never rely on anyone but yourself."

Another belief that rolled easily off his tongue, was: 'If you want to get the job done right, do it yourself."

Then of course, there were his two favourites, "Hard work never hurt anyone", and "All good things come to those who work, and wait."

Words, and beliefs, from a different generation, for a different generation.

Dad was an entrepreneur. And in his business success, I saw that what he said bore healthy fruit. From there, it was a logical step to accept that what he said, must be true. It made sense to me, and I absorbed the sense of it.

Yet the wisdom of his guidance, left me with the notion that I needed to be tough, in order to make it out in the world. And perhaps this is what evolved into an: 'I can forge ahead, and accomplish it, regardless' approach.

I can accomplish this. I can so do this. I can do this incredibly well. I'll show you just how able I am, and make you proud.

Ah yes, and there is that wanting-to-prove-worthiness vibration, again.

o   Wanting to prove your worthiness.

o   Wanting to prove your worth to another.

o   When the only relationship that ever matters, is your relationship with your Guiding-self.

This is a relationship based on the partnership of eternal love. This relationship does not ask anything of you. Has no expectation of you. In this relationship, you have nothing to prove. Your worthiness is truly and fully known.

That greater non-physical part of you, knows you to be an extension of the Creator-force. Knows you to be a part of the energy that creates worlds. And *this* is the wholeness of worthiness.

So it is, that when:

- You close the gap between you and you, through your vibrational alignment.

- Nothing else matters to you, other than you feeling good.

- You get to that place of knowing - not just thinking 'maybe', not just feeling 'it would be nice to be' - but knowing that you are an extension of this Creator-force.

Then, and only then, do you come to know – to fully understand, and to believe in, and to feel completely - the extent of your worthiness.

Your worthiness is magnificent. Your worthiness is sublime. Unparalleled in all of the universe.

Once you realize your worthiness. When you hold your head high, in solidly knowing your true value. Then you will fully embrace the fact that you truly deserve to receive all, and everything that your heart desires.

Now wouldn't it be nice if there was some way to ingrain that into our DNA, so we would always get to remember our true value.

YOU ARE NEVER ALONE

When you came into this physical body, you never intended to overcome challenges. Nor did you intend to struggle and suffer.

NONE of that is satisfying. None of that is fun. On the contrary: Struggle is deleting rather than replenishing. It's all about hardship rather than ease.

Struggle is about attracting that which you don't want, rather than attracting that which you do want. Suffering breaks-down, rather than builds-up. It's anxiety-provoking rather than rewarding. Struggle induces fear, rather than fostering eagerness. In a nutshell, struggle sucks.

On the other hand, nothing is more satisfying than alignment with your non-physical partner, and consciously co-creating.

This means allowing the Path of Greatest Ease, which is also the Path of Least Resistance, to reveal itself to you. And then, one-by-one, following the clues that light up along the way, through the continual broadcast offered by your Guiding-self.

This is why you came into physical form. To thrive. You came for the joy of intentional creation. You came for the joy of the expansion of the 'All' that you are.

You certainly did not intend to pinch yourself off from non-physical, and then crunch alone along the Path of Most Discord, that is also the Path of Most Resistance, that is over-shadowed by inevitable struggle.

You see, you never need to rely solely on yourself; on only this physical version of who you are. Because:

- It's deeply unsatisfying.

- You came into physical form, knowing that the greater part of you remained in non-physical form, with the express intention of partnering with you, in this eternal dance of co-creative expansion.

- You have access to the very energy that creates universes. And this energy is flowing to and through you, every minute of every day.

  Oh, did you feel that? This is a so huge:

  o   You have access to the energy that creates worlds.

  o   And all you need do, is to learn how to tune-in to it.

How powerful is that? How empowering is that? How amazing does this knowledge leave you feeling?

The knowledge that the very energy that creates worlds is flowing to you, and through you at all times. And all you need do, to live happily ever after, is to tune-in to it.

You see, Dad was onto something, but he only had hold of the tail of it. If he'd had access to the knowledge we have, he would have said:

- You can have, be and do anything you desire, through an understanding of the laws of the universe, and the eternal nature that you are.

- You can have, be and do anything you desire through an understanding that you are an extension of the energy that creates universes, in manifested form.

- You can have, be and do anything you desire through an understanding of, and practising of, lining-up with that part of you that is pure, positive energy.

- You can have, be and do anything you desire, through the understanding that your emotions act as a guidance system, that helps you accomplish this.

THE KEY, IS THE JOURNEY

You hold a set of beliefs that underpin the choices you make,
all day every day.

AND often, the habits of thought that you hold on each and every subject imaginable, lead you along a path of struggle. Because they contradict your desires.

These practised patterns of thinking are unique unto you, in their specificity, but are shared, in their generality. And the law of attraction lines you up with others that share these same practised patterns of thought, on different subjects. In this way momentum grows and the thoughts become more powerful, and manifestations occur.

Chances are, if you are resonating with those around you, or with any of the other constantly circulating streams of consciousness, you will not be aware of the promptings being offered by your Guiding-self. You'll be tuned-in somewhere else.

Yet despite this, in those times of pleasure, of relaxation, of calm, of meditation, of appreciation, of being in the zone, in fact many times during the day, you *do* unwittingly tune-in to the guidance that is always flowing to you.

Now, isn't it time for you to start doing so, with intent?

Ultimately, all that went before brings you to this very moment of expansion - to greater understanding, and to greater asking, and to greater receiving. Because expansion means 'More'.

- o   This is what you're all about: Wanting more. Always wanting more.

By deliberately tuning-in to the 'Whole' of who you are, you allow the energy of Creation to flow through you, to create more of what you desire through its constant revealing. And it will always be for the highest good, because this connection is pure Love.

Through your dominant vibration, you, and only you get to decide what works for you. And you will come to know, that in ease lies the revealing of what is desired. That through ease comes the greatest expansion into what is desired. That struggle is so unnecessary.

In fact, from this physical stand-point, struggle is an unadulterated waste of time. Literally. Because you get to do it all over again, and again, and again. And life really *is* meant to be fun.

That's what a reader once told me. She said "You came to have fun".

Back then, I couldn't make sense of that wisdom. I took the reference to 'fun' to mean the relationships, and the work, and the things with which we fill our lives. And yet, the pleasure in it all felt momentary. Short-lived. And the busy-ness, a distraction. Something was missing.

Today the world over, this feeling of 'a void within' is being widely experienced, and voiced. Many are awakening to an underlying sense of treading water. Waiting for some-thing that will bring meaning to, and make sense of it all.

Make sense of why you are here? And what you are really meant to be doing? And how to make your life more fulfilling?

What you need to know, is that in the very moment you birth each question, your attention on it ensures that the solution is generated vibrationally. And your acceptance of this, lies on your path to its physical unfolding.

However, when you continue day in and week out, to wonder why? Or how? Or when? When you keep trying to figure out who? Or what? Then your asking holds you in the vibration of the question. Thereby preventing you from receiving the answers you want. This is true of all questions. And of all problems. Regardless of their nature.

The void I felt for so long in searching for answers, no longer exists. The questioning has been filled with this knowledge:

You came into physical form to experience joyful expansion, through the conscious co-creation of all that you uniquely desire.

- The fun lies in choosing, and in focussing, and in aligning. And watching your life unfold in the way you specifically want it to. Unfold through your very own thoughts, imaginings, and inspired actions.

- Unbridled pleasure lies in acknowledging that this is all your doing. Every-thing. All of it. And that it is all yours to mould as you wish, in your very own unique way.

- Total satisfaction comes from consciously catching your emotions; adjusting your vibration to that which is higher; and then witnessing the results, as you just keep feeling better.

- The fun lies in taking the time to recognize every synchronicity, every rendezvous, every 'ah-ha' moment; in joining the dots as you receive the nudges, and then acting on these inspirations to deliberately create all you desire.

Yes indeed. This is the source of the fun the reader spoke of.

Pleasure is to be found in *every step* along the way of your joyful, intentional creating. In every step. In the journey itself.

Because every thought, and every idea; every feeling and every emotion; every unfolding, is a manifestation in itself. And every single manifestation is a source of joy, and excitement, and satisfaction for you. If you would only recognize, and realize this.

Your satisfaction is not all rolled up in one wad – in the final receiving of each of your desires. That's just the tail bit. That's the old news. By the time you get it, you've long since moved on from there. Now you're wanting more.

The real spine-tingling pleasure is there for your taking, in the *journey* to *that* which you are wanting. Therein lies the ease, and all the fulfilment, that you have been seeking.

This is why you came. This is your happily, ever after.

Truly.

WISH UPON A STAR

I leave you with an excerpt from a film I once saw.

I CANNOT recall the title, nor anything about the movie. But this moment of deliberate creation, that centred on a birthday celebration, stayed with me.

"When you wish for something, you announce to the universe that there's a hole in you that needs to be filled. And the more wishes you make, the more holes you open up.

There was a time in my life, when I was so filled with holes. Ah, I wished for a lot of things!

So, this is what I did. I stopped wishing, and I started saying 'thank you' for the things I already had. I started with the big things, like my friends, my family, my hair. And there were also little things, like the smile from a stranger, a strong cup of coffee, not hitting one red light on my way home.

Pretty soon, I was so filled with appreciation, there wasn't any room for holes. I crowded them all out.

Now, I don't make wishes. I want what I get".

❖ ❖ ❖ ❖ ❖ ❖

That's it, in a nutshell: Want what you get.

Don't just make a wish, and hope it comes true. Don't allow your dreams to rest on the wishful thinking of some magical wand somewhere being waved.

You have already created that beautiful life you're wishing for. Know that 'it *is*', rather than hope that 'it could be'.

And don't just take these words at face value. Try them out yourself. Make them part of your experience. Put them into practice for 30 days, and see what happens. Witness for yourself the changes you will observe. And then you'll want to practice them for another 30 days. And another. And more.

Because once you start to experience the magic [8] for yourself, you will come to believe in your happily, ever after. And then, expectation replaces hope. And in your positive expectation of your dreams being fulfilled, you realize your wishes.

You see, by creating with intent, you *can* master that magical wand, and direct the full magnificent force of it towards your own life.

You create through the ever-changing vibration you emanate. You create through what you broadcast. And, now that you are aware of this, there's no going back. You cannot undo the knowledge you have gained. Quite simply: You are wiser now than before.

---

[8] Deliberately creating is not magic. It's oh-so real. Yet, as you savour the fruits of your focus, it sure feels magical. Until you come to realize that each delicious step really *is* just the next logical step in your process of becoming.

And in no time at all, you come to experience the sense of joy in thinking: "Well, of course you'd do that for me. Much appreciated". And, "Of course that would happen for me, thank you".

So, stop creating by default, and this very day begin to create the joyful, prosperous, fulfilled life you've been dreaming of. Afterall, you *do* now know how.

Make a list of 'What I Enjoy'. Date your entry. Read it often. And add to it frequently. Use compliments freely. Treat yourself and all around you with compassion. And, remember to be easy on yourself.

Aim to feel good, and to have fun with all of this. Today and today and today and today. You see, creating is what you do. Magical, or not. It's yours to create.

So, go ahead. Wish upon a star. And in that moment, know you are the both the Manifester of, and the Receiver of all that you Wish for.

Now, *that* is true empowerment.

Afterword

About the Author P. A. Pilio.

MY journey has, like that of many others, led me from one discipline to another, from one area of discovery to another, from one source to another. And, typically, has been 'mile-stoned' by personal challenge. It is as if each new chapter reveals a little more, and so I keep seeking.

Because, from my earliest memory, I knew there had to be more. And once I opened the door to Abraham, clarity avalanched in. I started unravelling and piecing together complexities gleaned through the years. And although from widely different sources and disciplines, there is no ending to their dovetailing.

I have always felt part of a Spiritual team, yet that team never felt quite within reach. There was always a barrier of sorts. Them 'up there', literally and figuratively, and me 'down here'. Like being caught between a rock and a hard place. Wanting to feel empowered, yet feeling small. And, this goes to the heart of a feeling of unworthiness. To a sense that being in physical form is somehow lesser than.

When in reality, we are a partnership. You get to choose the 'what'. And then, the greater part of you that remained in non-physical, that knows in every moment just what to do, leads you ever-forward, to your mutual expansion. A work-in-progress, as it were.

There is no Creator sitting in judgement. Instead, the Creator-force flows unceasingly, to and through each one of us. In symphony, you can create the life you want with intention, and then watch the truth of that unfold.

I realize that each and every one of the situations I have experienced, had, and has, *nothing* to do with 'lessons to be learnt', nor about karma. Rather, each was, and has been, about deliberate expansion through oftentimes, un-deliberate creation.

I consider myself truly blessed in the diversity of my guidance. And I take such pleasure witnessing, moment-by-moment, my alignment with my Guiding-self. Or not. And then, in my deliberate adjustment, the yielding of the Universe, as I find myself in a place of expanding equilibrium and joy.

May it be so for you, too.
And, so it is.

P.A. Pilio

Acknowledgements

With such Appreciation and Love, to:

ABRAHAM and Esther Hicks, whose teachings are the gift that just keeps on giving. Seth and Jane Roberts, who blazed the modern trail. The Archangels, the Ascended Masters, and Council of 12, for their unceasing prodding. Madam Blavatsky and others in the Theosophical tradition for an initiation into new thinking. Marc and Elizabeth Clare Prophet and the Summit Lighthouse, for their powerful believing. The Radiant Rose Academy and Usha, for the teachings of Akasha. Kabbalist Jacobus Swart for his 'Shadow Tree' trilogy, and Hadassah Fine who helped me with the language. Master Babaji and Jeanine Strong for years of insight. Jackie Brooke, my teacher in the Tradition of Astrology. Kryon and Lee Carroll for answers in the early days. The Dali Llama and other Buddhist Masters, for their Inner knowing and powerful chanting. And so many others: sages, psychologists, scholars, theorists and scientists, whose writings and insights have inspired.

Bran, without whom publishing would not have been possible. A heartfelt thank you for your patience throughout production. Michelle Vooght, fellow traveller, and remarkable angel-reader. Col and Sim for never doubting. Mal for your valuable insight. Pips, Pierre G and John M, for your unwavering support.

Thank-you, one and all

About the Author

THESE are the first thoughts-turned-to-words presented to you, by P.A.Pilio.

More will follow.

Should you wish to contact the author, we look forward to hearing from you:

Email:

author@papilio.uk

Website:

www.papilio.uk